REA

ACPL ITEM
DISCARDED

SO-BWY-387

7-1-63

SAINTS, SIGNS, AND SYMBOLS

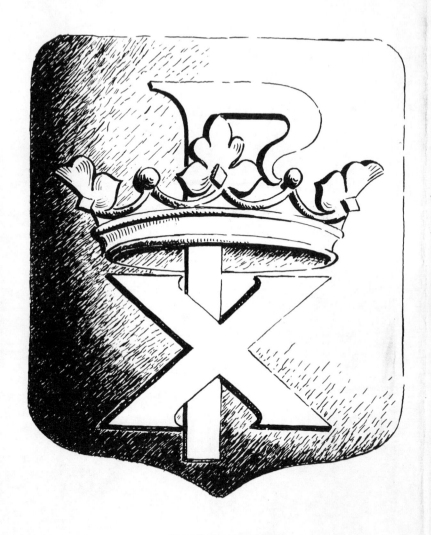

CHRIST THE KING

A symbol composed of the Chi Rho and
crown. The crown and Chi are gold with
Rho of silver on a blue field.

SAINTS, SIGNS
and
SYMBOLS

by

W. ELLWOOD POST

Illustrated by the author

Foreword by

The Rev. EDWARD N. WEST, D.D.
Canon Sacrist
The Cathedral Church of St. John the Divine,
New York

MOREHOUSE-BARLOW CO.
NEW YORK

© 1962 by Morehouse-Barlow Co.
Library of Congress Catalogue Card No. 62-19257

Printed in the United States of America

1237557

Foreword

Ellwood Post's book is a genuine addition to the ecclesiological library. It contains a monumental mass of material which is not ordinarily available in one book—particularly if the reader must depend in general on the English language.

Books in this field are, too often, either written brilliantly and illustrated badly, or *vice versa*. This book contains some excellent drawing combined with the most terse descriptive writing possible. It will prove to be a most practical reference work for all those who deal with the Church's symbols, and it will add vastly to the information of those who already know much of this science.

The reader who is unacquainted with the language of symbols must approach the subject with the clear understanding that "naturalism" is the exact opposite of "symbolism." Once this is understood, the criterion of judgment on the effectiveness of any particular symbol and the suitability of its portrayal is firmly established. On such a basis, this book is important.

EDWARD N. WEST

Acknowledgments

To the Rev. Dr. Edward N. West, Canon Sacrist of the Cathedral Church of St. John the Divine, New York, who has graciously given of his scholarly knowledge and fatherly encouragement, I express my sincere gratitude. Also, I wish to tender my thanks to the Rev. Frank V. H. Carthy, Canon Almoner of Christ Church Cathedral and Rector of All Saints' Parish, Indianapolis, Indiana, who initiated my interest in the drama of the Church; and to my wife, Bette, for her loyal cooperation.

The research material used has been invaluable, and I am indebted to writers, past and contemporary. They are: E. E. Dorling, *Heraldry of the Church;* Arthur Charles Fox-Davies, *Guide to Heraldry;* Shirley C. Hughson of the Order of the Holy Cross, *Athletes of God;* Dr. F. C. Husenbeth, *Emblems of Saints;* C. Wilfrid Scott-Giles, *The Romance of Heraldry;* and F. R. Webber, *Church Symbolism.*

W. ELLWOOD POST

Contents

Introduction

This book is confined to illustrations of symbols used in the Church, along with identification and brief notes relative to color or traditional legends. Canon West has furnished the colors suggested as well as some of the designs. Space permits only one illustration for each saint, though there are usually several symbols by which that saint is known.

It is the purpose of this book to acquaint the reader with these emblems and relate them to fact or legend in simple terms. Visual aids prove helpful to teachers, pupils, and those engaged in parish efforts to beautify the Church.

The ancient heralds expressed their messages with clean firm lines, good balance, proportion, and splendor of color. This form of art has played an important role in the Church through the centuries, due to its ability to bring into focus important persons and facts in her history.

Acquaint yourself with the symbols that follow and go a step farther, too. Obtain reading material so that you may, even more fully, relate the symbol to the life of the person or event represented. A broader knowledge, and interest in efforts to make the House of God more beautiful for him, should be the aim of all Churchmen.

COLOR

It is recommended that heraldic colors be clean, strong, and harmonious. For example:

Red: Use clear bright scarlet, not pink or terra-cotta.
Green: Use vivid spring green, such as the color of grass or jade, not olive or emerald.
Blue: Use Prussian blue, not hot purply blue.

A general rule of heraldry is the avoidance of color on color or metal on metal. Gold and silver, referred to as "or" and "argent" in heraldic terminology, are metals. Golden yellow may be substituted for gold and white used in place of silver. The forementioned rule appears to have some exceptions, as is also true of certain colors, where their meaning is apparently lost. Students and scholars of the science hold to the original colors, in order to maintain tradition.

Following are generally accepted interpretations of the significance of colors, as used by the Church:

Black	Solemnity, negation, sickness, death.
Black and white	Humility, purity of life.
Blue	Heavenly love, unveiling of truth. Traditional color of St. Mary, the Blessed Virgin. In the English Scheme of Liturgical Colors, blue is used in Advent and on the Pre-Lenten 'Gesima Sundays.
Brown	Renunciation of the world, spiritual death and degradation.
Gold	See white.
Gray	Ashes, humility, mourning.
Green	Spring, triumph of life over death, charity, regeneration of soul through good works, hope. Epiphany and Trinity seasons.
Purple	Royalty, imperial power (God the Father).
Red	Martyred saints, love, hate, sovereign power. Pentecost.
Violet	Love, truth, passion, suffering. In the western use, Advent and Lent.
White (Gold)	Innocence of soul, purity, holiness of life. Christmas, The Epiphany, Easter, The Ascension, Trinity Sunday, the Transfiguration, All Saints, etc.
Yellow	Dingy: Infernal light, degradation, jealousy, treason, deceit.

Religious Orders are sometimes represented by the colors of their habits.

Black	The Benedictines, Augustinians, Jesuits, Cowley Fathers.
Gray	The Franciscans. Dark brown if the reformed branch.
White	The reformed branch of the Benedictines, Cistercians, Praemonstratensians, the Order of the Holy Cross.
Black over white	The Dominicans.
White over brown	The Carmelites.

Abbreviations

Ap.	Apostle	H.	Hermit
Ab.	Abbot	K.	King
Abs.	Abbess	M.	Martyr
Ar.	Archbishop	P.	Pope
B.	Bishop	Pen.	Penitent
C.	Confessor	Q.	Queen
Car.	Cardinal	St.	Saint
D.	Doctor	V.	Virgin
Dc.	Deacon	W.	Widow
Emp.	Emperor	c.	about
Eps.	Empress	cen.	century
Ev.	Evangelist		

Note: Dates are shown
by century and are to
be understood as A. D.

The Four Evangelists

ST. MATTHEW THE EVANGELIST, ►
AP.M. — The emblem of the "Divine Man" was assigned to St. Matthew in ancient times because his Gospel teaches us about the human nature of Christ. A gold angel on a red field.

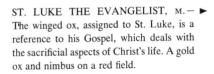

◄ ST. MARK THE EVANGELIST, M. — The winged lion, ancient symbol of St. Mark, refers to his Gospel, which informs us of the royal dignity of Christ. A gold winged lion and nimbus on a red field.

ST. LUKE THE EVANGELIST, M. — ►
The winged ox, assigned to St. Luke, is a reference to his Gospel, which deals with the sacrificial aspects of Christ's life. A gold ox and nimbus on a red field.

◄ ST. JOHN THE EVANGELIST, AP. — The ancient symbol of a rising eagle is said to have been assigned to St. John because his gaze pierced further into the mysteries of Heaven than that of any man. The manner of his death is not known. A gold eagle rising and nimbus on a blue field.

The Twelve Apostles

◄ ST. ANDREW, AP.M., 1st cen. — The patron of Russia, Scotland, and the Ecumenical Patriarchate. According to tradition St. Andrew was crucified on an X shaped cross, known as a saltire or St. Andrew's cross, in Achaia. A silver saltire on a blue field.

ST. BARTHOLOMEW, AP.M., 1st cen. — ► Armenia and India are believed to have been the areas of his missionary work. He is said to have been flayed alive and crucified. Flaying knives with silver blades and gold handles, on a red field.

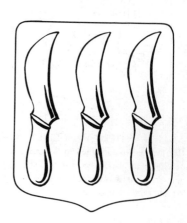

◄ ST. JAMES THE GREATER, AP.M., 1st cen. — The patron of Spain and of pilgrims. He is mentioned as the first of the disciples to go on a missionary journey. The escallop shells refer to pilgrimage. Three gold shells on a blue field.

The Twelve Apostles

ST. JAMES THE LESS, AP.M., 1st cen. — ►
This symbol refers to the tradition that St.
James was cast down from a pinnacle of
the temple in Jerusalem, stoned and sawn
asunder by the Jews. A saw with silver
blade and gold handle, on a red field.

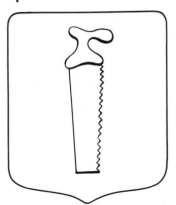

◄ ST. JOHN, AP.EV., 1st cen. — This emblem
of St. John, the "Beloved Apostle," refers
to the legend of a poisoned chalice being
offered to him, in an attempt made on his
life. A gold chalice, a silver serpent, on a
blue field.

ST. JUDE, AP.M., 1st cen. — The sailing ►
vessel here represents the Church, which
St. Jude (also known as Thaddeus or Leb-
baeus) carried to many ports as he jour-
neyed as a missionary. A gold ship with
silver sails, on a red field.

The Twelve Apostles

◄ ST. MATTHEW, AP.EV.M., 1st cen. — The moneybags refer to the occupation of St. Matthew before he was called to follow Christ. He was a tax gatherer known as Levi. Silver moneybags, on a red field.

ST. MATTHIAS, AP.M., 1st cen. — Chosen, ► by lot, to replace Judas Iscariot, St. Matthias served as a missionary in Judaea, where he is said to have been stoned and beheaded. A battle axe with silver head and tawny handle, white open book with inscription "super Mathiam" in black except the upper case "M", of red, all on a red field.

◄ ST. PETER, AP.M., 1st cen. — Because he felt unworthy to die as had Christ, St. Peter requested that his cross be inverted so that he might look Heavenward as he was crucified. A gold cross, silver keys of the Kingdom of Heaven, all on a red field.

The Twelve Apostles

ST. PHILIP, AP.M., 1st cen. — It was to St. ▶
Philip that Christ addressed his remark
concerning the feeding of the multitude.
(St. John 6, 7). The roundels represent two
loaves of bread. A gold cross, silver roundels, on a red field.

◀ ST. SIMON, AP.M., 1st cen. — The com-
panion of St. Jude on many missionary
journeys, St. Simon was known as a great
fisher of men through the power of the Gospel. A gold Book, page edges of white, silver fish, all on a red field.

ST. THOMAS, AP.M., 1st cen. — The pa- ▶
tron of builders. He is said to have built a
Church with his own hands in East India.
The spear refers to the instrument of his
martyrdom. A carpenter's square with silver blade and gold handle, spear with silver
head and tawny handle, all on a red field.

◀ JUDAS ISCARIOT, 1st cen. — Thirty
pieces of silver with a straw colored rope
on a black field.

15

The Holy Trinity

TREFOIL

TRIQUETRA

Shown above is the doctrine of the Blessed Trinity as clearly expressed by the early armorists. It is fitting that this symbol be borne on shield or banner by churches dedicated to the Holy Trinity. The emblem is silver with black legend, on a red field.

CIRCLE WITHIN TRIANGLE

EQUILATERAL TRIANGLE

TRIANGLE IN CIRCLE

TRIQUETRA AND CIRCLE

THE THREE FISHES

INTERWOVEN CIRCLES

God the Father

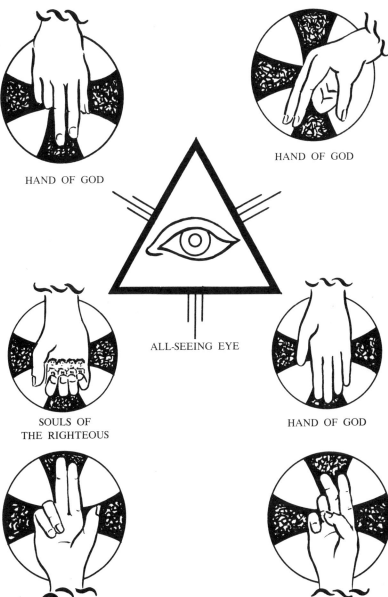

HAND OF GOD

HAND OF GOD

ALL-SEEING EYE

SOULS OF
THE RIGHTEOUS

HAND OF GOD

HAND OF GOD
(Latin Form)

HAND OF GOD
(Greek Form)

17

God the Son

AGNUS DEI (The Lamb of God) with the Banner of Victory — St. John, having baptized Jesus Christ, said, "Behold the Lamb of God which taketh away the sin of the world." Ref. The Gospel of St. John 1:29 and 36, Revelation 5:13, and I Corinthians 5:7.

A white lamb with gold nimbus showing three red rays, and a red cross upon a white banner supported by a silver staff with a gold cross at the top, all on a blue field.

THE FISH — A Christian symbol used from the first century. The Greek word for fish, ΙΧΘΥΣ upon which a rebus was made, is derived from the first letters of Ιησους Χριστὸς Θεοῦ Υἱός Σωτήρ "Jesus Christ, Son of God, Saviour."

AGNUS DEI AND THE BOOK OF SEVEN SEALS — The Lamb of God who alone is "Worthy to receive power, wealth and wisdom and might and honor and glory and blessings." Ref. Revelation 5:12.

THE PHOENIX — A legendary bird, used in early times as a symbol of the Resurrection.

THE FOUNTAIN — "On that day there shall be a fountain opened for the house of David and the inhabitants of Jerusalem to cleanse them from sin and uncleanness." Ref. Zechariah 13:1. (The heraldic form is shown.)

God the Holy Spirit

THE DESCENDING DOVE—A white dove, of conventional design, with three rayed nimbus, is the most appropriate traditional symbol of the Holy Spirit. Ref. St. Luke 3:21-22—"Now when all the people were baptized, and when Jesus also had been baptized and was praying, the heaven was opened, and the Holy Spirit descended upon him in bodily form, as a dove, and a voice came from heaven, 'Thou art my beloved Son; with thee I am well pleased.'" Further Ref. St. Matthew 3:16, St. Mark 1:10, St. John 1:32.

THE SEVENFOLD FLAME—The tongues of fire, a symbol of the power of the Holy Spirit as mentioned by St. Luke in The Acts of The Apostles 2:1-4.

THE SEVEN LAMPS—The gifts of the Holy Spirit which are:

Wisdom	Ghostly strength
Understanding	Knowledge
Counsel	True godliness

Holy fear

The Sacred Monograms

The use of certain groups of letters, derived from Greek and Latin words, as symbols of our Lord Jesus Christ was instituted in the early days of the Christian Church. For example, the monograms illustrated are based on the Greek words:

IHCOYC meaning Jesus.

It was from IHCOYC that the familiar IHC was derived. This form of the monogram is preferred over IHS because of its date of origin.

XPICTOC meaning Christ. The Chi Rho is composed of the first two letters of XPICTOC.

NIKA meaning Victor.

The familiar first and last letters of the Greek alphabet, Alpha and Omega (A and Ω), used in the Christian Church, denote the eternity and infinitude of God. The Alpha-Omega emblem is often used in conjunction with another symbol, such as a cross or crown, etc. to emphasize this meaning.

INRI The Latin words, "Iesus Nazarenus Rex Iudaeorum," or "Jesus of Nazareth, the King of the Jews," which was written over the Cross of Christ, is represented by INRI.

Note: A horizontal, slightly curved line over the letters indicates abbreviation.

IHC WITH CROWN

JESUS CHRIST VICTOR

IHC IN LATIN FORM

IHC IN LATIN FORM

IHC IN LATIN FORM

The Sacred Monograms

CHI RHO

CHI RHO

CHI RHO with NIKA or
NOSTER, Latin for Our Christ

CHI RHO

CHI RHO AND GREEK CROSS

CHI RHO WITH GREEK CROSS

The Sacred Monograms

CHI RHO WITH ANCHOR CROSS
(From the catacombs)
AND ALPHA AND OMEGA

CHI RHO WITH ALPHA AND
OMEGA

ALPHA AND OMEGA
AND ANCHOR CROSS
(Eternal Hope)

ALPHA AND OMEGA
WITH CROWN
(The Lord)

CHI RHO SIGMA OF CHRIST

JESUS OF NAZARETH,
THE KING OF THE JEWS

St. Mary the Virgin

ST. MARY the Virgin, 1st cen. — This emblem, suggestive of Mater dolorosa, is a reference to the words of Simeon, "Yea, a sword shall pass through thine own soul also."

Colors

A red heart with gold wings and pierced by a silver sword with gold hilt, on a field of blue, the Virgin's color.

THE LILY — A symbol of virginity and purity.

THE FLEUR-DE-LYS — A symbol of the Holy Trinity which is also used as a symbol of the Blessed Virgin, because of its derivation from the Madonna's lily.

THE MYSTIC ROSE — Illustrated in its preferable heraldic form.

THE MONOGRAM OF THE BLESSED VIRGIN — The letters of the name "Maria" are evident in this ancient symbol. A crown was sometimes placed over the monogram by Medieval artists.

THE MATER DEI — This abbreviated form refers to St. Mary as the Mother of God.

THE CRESCENT MOON — Shown in its proper position and form, the crescent moon is significant of the glory of the Virgin Mother as borrowed from her son, Jesus Christ, the Sun of Righteousness, even as the moon reflects the sun.

Saints

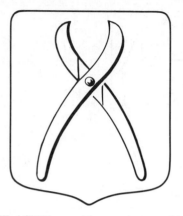

◀ ST. AGATHA, V.M., 3rd cen. — During the Decian persecution, St. Agatha, a Sicilian of noble birth, died under torture rather than break her vow of lifelong consecration to Christ. Gold pincers on a red field.

ST. AGNES, V.M., 4th cen. — A young girl ▶ who refused to abandon her practice of the Christian Faith and therefore suffered death at the time of the Diocletian persecution. This symbol expresses her sacrifice for the Faith. White lamb, gold book, on a red field.

◀ ST. AIDAN, B.C., 7th cen. — A monk of Iona chosen to evangelize the northern English, and consecrated Bishop of Lindisfarne. This emblem was assigned to St. Aidan for his ability to enlighten through the power of the Gospel. Gold torch with red flames tipped white, on a blue field.

ST. ALBAN, M., 4th cen. — The first British martyr ('Protomartyr Anglorum') and the abbey at Hartfordshire dedicated in his honor, bear the same arms. A gold saltire on a blue field.

Saints

ST. ALPHEGE, AR.M., 11th cen. (St. Aelf-heah, St. Elphage) — The twenty-seventh Archbishop of Canterbury, who in an attempt to defend his cathedral city against the invading Danes, was captured and tortured. A soldier, filled with pity, ended the life of St. Alphege with his battle axe. Gold axe-head on silver handle, and field of red.

ST. ANNE, 1st cen. — The mother of St. Mary the Virgin, whose loving care of her daughter is shown by the silver border masoned in black. The silver lily on a blue field refers to the girlhood of the Virgin.

◄ ST. AMBROSE, B.C.D., 4th cen. — The scourges represent the strict discipline of the Bishop of Milan. The beehive refers to his eloquence as he labored to maintain and clarify the need for proper respect of the Church. He assisted in the conversion of St. Augustine and baptized him. Gold beehive, silver scourges on a blue field.

◄ ST. ANSELM, AR.C.D., 12th cen. — Writer of the Christian classic, "Cur Deus Homo." This thirty-fourth Archbishop of Canterbury, amid difficulties with royalty, guarded the spiritual independence of the Church (represented by the ship symbol). Gold ship, silver sails, white pennants with red crosses, white waves on a blue field.

Saints

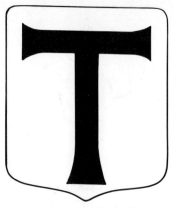

◄ ST. ANTONY OF EGYPT, AB.H.C., 4th cen. (St. Anthony) — The ancient Egyptian symbol, the Tau cross, refers to the desert monastery founded by St. Antony, who, earlier in life, disposed of his wealth to pursue the solitary life of devotion to Christ. Silver Tau cross on a black field.

ST. ANTONY OF PADUA, C., 13th cen. ► (St. Anthony) — A member of the Order of St. Francis, whose phenomenal knowledge of Holy Scripture, as indicated by the Book, combined with his eloquence, earned him the honor of being called "The eldest son of St. Francis." He died at the age of twenty-six. The lilies refer to his purity, the stems to his youth. Gold Book, silver lilies with green stems, on a brown field.

ST. ASAPH, c. 6th cen. — There is no reason known for the assignment of this emblem to the Prior of Llan-Elwyn, a follower of St. Kentigern. The two keys have been used traditionally, as they were engraved ◄ in the seal of Robert Lancaster, the Bishop of St. Asaph, 1411-1433. Other examples substitute a crozier for one key. Silver keys on a black field.

ST. ATHANASIUS, AR.C.D., 4th cen. — ► The symbols shown indicate both the great Greek Father's defence of Orthodoxy, and his episcopal office. The triangle is gold, the pallium white with black crosses and black decoration, all on a blue field.

Saints

ST. AUGUSTINE OF CANTERBURY, A.R.C., 7th cen. — Missionary to the Engles, member of the Benedictine Order, and the ▶ first Archbishop of Canterbury, is assigned the cross and pall to indicate his archepiscopal rank. The lily of the Madonna is believed to have been included because he died in May, the month of Mary. Silver cross, gold pall, silver lily, on a black field.

◀ ST. AUGUSTINE OF HIPPO, B.C.D., 5th cen. — A native of North Africa, converted by St. Ambrose and educated at Carthage, the Bishop of Hippo was the writer of his "Confessions" and "The City of God." This symbol refers to his intense zeal and devotion to Christ. Gold heart aflame, on a blue field.

ST. BARBARA OF HELIOPOLIS, V.M., c. 4th cen. — The patron of the Artillery ▶ and of those who follow dangerous trades. Legend relates that her father imprisoned her in a tower which was broken open by a bolt of lightning. Silver castle with gold streak of lightning, on a red field.

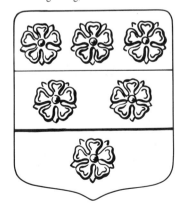

◀ ST. BARNABAS, AP.M., 1st cen. — One of the Apostolic Fathers, whose feast day in olden times was celebrated by young lads and clerks bedecked with roses. This shield is divided. Top and bottom rows are silver Tudor roses on a red field. The center row bears red roses on a silver field.

Saints

ST. BEDE, C., 8th cen. — One of the great ► men of faith (to which this emblem refers), writer of the first ecclesiastical history of England and the first to translate the Bible into English. He is referred to as the "Venerable Bede" in his epitaph. Gold pitcher with the light from Heaven indicated by silver rays emanating from the gold center, on a blue field.

ST. BERNARD OF CLAIRVAUX, AB., 12th cen. — Founded 163 Cistercian mon- ► asteries, assisted at innumerable peace Councils, preached a Crusade in France and Germany and wrote many treatises and sermons. Three white mitres with gold bands, and a gold book, refer both to his writing, and to the fact that he was offered a bishopric three times. The field is blue.

◄ ST. BASIL THE GREAT, B.C.D., 4th cen. — One of the Greek Fathers, Bishop of Caeserea, and brother to SS. Gregory of Nyssa and Peter of Sebaste, was a prolific writer and defender of the doctrine of the Incarnation of Jesus Christ. The emblem refers to his building up the Church. A gold Byzantine church on a blue field.

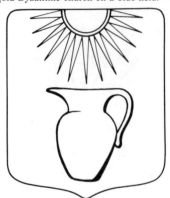

ST. BENEDICT OF NURSIA, AB., 6th cen. — The Father of Western Monasticism left to the monks of his Order his Famous Rule. A gold sword with hilt forming a ◄ cross, white scroll tipped red, with red inscription, "The cross of the holy father." (Benediciti is a play on the word Benedict.) All on a black field.

Saints

ST. BLASIUS OF SEBASTE, B.M., 4th ►
cen. — (St. Blaise) Known as the patron of
wool-combers, legend relates that he was
tortured with the implement of their trade.
It was the custom in England to celebrate
the feast of St. Blasius until the early nine-
teenth century. Silver wool-comb on a red
field.

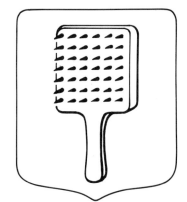

ST. BONIFACE, AR.M., 8th cen. — The ►
Archbishop of Mentz established the foun-
dation for Christianity in Germany. His
emblem refers to his defense of the Gospel
as he met the blow of death while con-
firming baptized converts. A gold Book,
sword with gold hilt and silver blade, on a
red field.

◄ ST. BONAVENTURE, B.C.D., 14th cen.
— A Minister General of the Franciscan
Order, distinguished for his scholarly ability and saintly manner, who was elevated
to the Office of a Cardinal. Gold cross and
chalice with the white Host displayed, on a
blue field.

◄ ST. BOTULPH, AB., 7th cen. (St. Botolph)
— A Benedictine abbey established by St.
Botulph at Ikanhoe, England, is represented here by the chevron and cross, indi-
cating, possibly, that he was a builder of a
sacred structure. The waves represent the
water about his dwelling. (Ikanhoe, later
called St. Botulphstown, was included in
Boston.) A black chevron and cross, on a
blue field with silver waves.

Saints

◀ ST. BRIGID OF KILDARE, v.abs., 6th cen. (St. Bride) — It is said that the nuns of the convent she founded kept a fire burning in memory of her. However, it may be inferred that this emblem refers to her good works, while the oak wreath represents Kildare. White was the color of her habit. A red lamp, green wreath, on a white field.

ST. CATHERINE OF ALEXANDRIA, ▶ v.q.m., 4th cen. — Patron of chastity and learning. The wheel set with spikes refers to that mentioned in the legend, which is said to have been broken by divine interposition, when persecutors attempted to break her upon it. A silver wheel on a blue field.

ST. CATHERINE OF SIENA, v., 14th ◀ cen. — Among many diplomatic achievements, St. Catherine is known for effecting a reconciliation between the Florentine people and the Papacy. This emblem refers to her faith and charitableness. A red cross, gold heart, on a black field.

ST. CECILIA, v.m., 3rd cen. — The only ▶ apparent reason for her to be known as the patroness of music is that St. Cecilia is said to have been skilled in singing the divine praises, oft accompanied by an instrument. A gold harp with silver strings, on a blue field.

Saints

ST. CHAD, B.C., 7th cen. (St. Ceadda) ►
— The Bishop of Mercia is regarded as the
missionary who introduced Christianity to
the East Saxons. His symbol, as used at
Lichfield, England, is quite unusual. The
sections shown as black in the illustration
are red, and the white sections are silver.

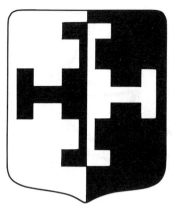

ST. CHARLES BORROMEO, AR.CAR.,
◄ 16th cen. — Though born to wealth and
prestige, the Archbishop of Milan was
venerated for his wisdom and humility.
These qualities were most helpful in en-
abling him to break the force of the reformation in Italy and Switzerland. Gold
crown, silver inscription, on a blue field.

ST. CHRISTOPHER, M., 3rd cen. — A
martyr of the Decian persecution was ►
called "Christopher," which means "Christ
bearer" in its Greek form. His emblem refers to one of many legends. The lamp refers to St. Christopher carrying Christ, the
Light of the World, to safety, and bearing
a staff which bloomed in one night. A silver lantern, gold staff, on a red field.

ST. CHRYSOSTOM (JOHN), AR.C.D.,
◄ 5th cen. — The great work of the Archbishop of Constantinople to overcome
crime, heresy, and corruption was inter-
rupted by avaricious enemies who effected
his exile, which lasted four years, and
ended with his death. A gold chalice upon
a gold Book, bordered silver, with a red
bookmark, bordered gold, on a blue field.

31

Saints

◄ ST. CLARE, v.abs., 13th cen. — The foundress of the Order of the Poor Clares, whose emblem refers to her dispersing Saracen invaders by facing them, bearing the Blessed Sacrament, in defense of the convent. Gold ciborium on a brown field.

ST. CLEMENT, b.m., 1st cen. — St. Paul ► mentioned the name of this Bishop of Rome as one of those whose names are written in the book of life. Banished under the persecution of Trajan, he continued to minister to his fellow Christians, for which he was condemned, bound to an anchor and cast into the sea. A gold anchor on a blue field.

ST. COLUMBA, ab., 6th cen. — The founder of the island sanctuary of Iona. He and ◄ the monks of his community performed a great work, evangelizing and ministering to the people of Scotland and northern England. A blue Iona cross on a white field.

ST. CORNELIUS, p.m., 3rd cen. — Although he successfully overcame the here- ► sies of Novation, he was exiled under Gallus. He is said to have died by the sword. The emblems are traditional. A gold cross, brown horn, on a red field.

Saints

ST. CUTHBERT, B.C, 7th cen. — The Bishop of Lindisfarne, later transferred to ▶ Durham, whose arms are thought to have been suggested by those of Durham, with a cross of different form and the color of the charges reversed. A gold cross, silver lions, on a blue field.

ST. CYRIL OF ALEXANDRIA, AR.C.D., 5th cen. — He is assigned two pens, referring to his divine authorship, and the ▶ Greek inscription meaning, "God-bearer," for his defense of the Blessed Virgin as upheld by the Church against the false doctrine of Nestorius. Gold pens, white scroll with black inscription, on a blue field.

◀ ST. CYPRIAN OF CARTHAGE, B.M., 3rd cen. — The Bishop of Carthage was an orator and scholar. Though converted to Christianity at an advanced age, he progressed rapidly to his high office, which he filled with sincerity. He was beheaded by order of Valerian. A silver double battle axe with head of silver and tawny handle, gold crown, on a red field.

ST. CYRIL OF JERUSALEM, B.C., 4th ◀ cen. — The Bishop of Jerusalem, a teacher and scholar, who triumphed in his struggle against Arian doctrines. The moneybag refers to a story that he sold the ornaments of the church to provide food for the poor. Gold moneybag, on a green field.

Saints

ST. DENYS, B.M., 1st cen. (St. Denis, St. ▶
Dennis, or St. Dionysius the Aeropagite.)
— This emblem is said to have been the
ensign of St. Denys, the reputed author of
the great mystical books. The Middle Ages
accepted it that he was martyred at the
hands of pagans, in the area of Paris. A
silver cross and lions, on a red field.

ST. DOMINIC, AB., 13th cen. — Founder ▶
of the Dominican Order, known as the
Friar Preachers, whose members came to
be known as "The watch dogs of the Lord,
defending the fold of the Church with the
fire of the Holy Spirit." A gray dog, brown
torch, red flames with white tips, on a
black and white field as illustrated, the
colors of the habit of the Dominican Order.

◄ ST. DAVID OF THESSALONICA, H.,
7th cen. — One of the two symbols asso-
ciated with this famous and, in his own
day, extremely popular hermit-saint is a
seated lion gazing out directly, silver, on a
black field.

ST. DAVID OF WALES, B.AB., 6th cen.
— A reference to the legend of St. David.
A vast assembly at a synod of Welsh bish-
◄ ops could not hear an important procla-
mation. When David was requested to
speak, the ground where he stood arose,
forming a mount, while a white dove
perched on his shoulder and his voice was
heard. A white dove with gold nimbus,
blue pile, green mount, all on a silver field.

ST. DOROTHY, V.M., 4th cen. — (St. Dorothea) The patroness of gardens is particularly well known in the little villages of southern Europe. The symbol shown was selected because it is descriptive of her zeal for the Faith. A gold torch, red flames with white tips, on a red field. ►

ST. EDWARD THE CONFESSOR, K.AB., 11th cen. — The founder of Westminster Abbey. These arms were designed for him long after his death. The martlets are thought to have been suggested by the birds that appeared on Edward's coins, ► representing the doves which stood at the top of his sceptre. A gold cross and martlets, on a blue field.

◄ ST. DUNSTAN, AR.C., 10th cen. — The Abbot of Glastonbury, later made the twenty-third Archbishop of Canterbury, St. Dunstan was sought by many eminent people for counsel. Through his efforts, respect for the Church was strengthened, and education of the people was advanced morally and intellectually. As a gifted artist he became the patron saint of goldsmiths. A gold covered cup, on a blue field.

◄ ST. EDMUND OF EAST ANGLIA, K.M., 9th cen. — King Edmund was a humble man and strove to secure peace for his people. He courageously faced the Danes, refusing to forsake the Faith or his people, and was slain by arrows. A gold crown and arrows, on a blue field.

35

Saints

ST. ELIZABETH, 1st cen. — The Maltese ►
cross represents the fruit of this vine, St.
John Baptist. The two withered leaves at
the base of the stem refer to the unfertility
of St. Elizabeth in earlier years. A silver
cross with gold stem and leaves, on a black
field.

ST. ERIC OF SWEDEN, K.M., 12th cen. ►
— Faith, mercy and justice are the attri-
butes of St. Eric, as shown in his dealing
with the Finns. He met his martyrdom at
the hands of malcontents who had con-
spired with the Prince of Denmark. Three
gold crowns, a fountain — waves of silver
and blue, on a red field.

◄ ST. EDWARD THE MARTYR, K.M.,
10th cen. — At the age of twelve years
Edward succeeded to the throne. He was
stabbed in the back by members of his step-
mother's household, as he accepted a prof-
fered cup of wine. A gold crown, sceptre
with gold head and silver staff, sword with
silver blade and gold hilt, all on a red field.

ST. ELIZABETH OF HUNGARY,
W.Q.C., 13th cen. — The three crowns refer
◄ to the blessedness of St. Elizabeth as a virgin, wife, and widow, as well as her rank.
She is said to have found solace throughout
her life, by faith, prayer, and ministering
to the unfortunate. Three gold crowns, on
a brown field.

Saints

ST. ETHELDREDA, v.q.abs., 7th cen. ▶
(St. Audrey) — An abbess of the monastery for men and women at Ely. She was installed by St. Wilfrid, and St. Cuthbert was numbered among her many friends. Her faith and charity are said to have been exemplary. Three gold crowns on a red field.

ST. FELICITAS, w.m., 3rd cen. (St. Felicity) — The maid of St. Perpetua, who for the Faith, met death with her mistress, during the persecution of Severus. Her ▶ babe was born while she was imprisoned. St. Augustine referred to the loyal maid and her mistress as, "Perpetual Felicity." Gold sword hilts with silver blades, on a red field.

◀ ST. FAITH, v.m., 3rd cen. — The courage and example of St. Faith when she was put to death for refusing to deny her belief in Christ, effected the conversion of others who witnessed the spectacle. Assigned to her is the symbol of the Faith, the Holy Trinity, but with different colors. A gold emblem inscribed with black, on a blue field.

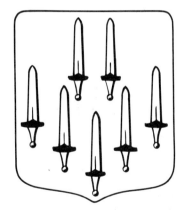

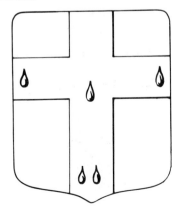

◀ ST. FRANCIS OF ASSISI, c., 13th cen. — It is said that St. Francis, the father of the Franciscan Order, for two years before his death bore the marks of the Lord's Passion upon his hands, feet and side. A silver cross, red marks of the stigmata, on a brown field.

Saints

ST. FRANCIS DE SALES, B.C.D., 17th cen. — The Bishop of Geneva, well loved for his gentleness and moderation, followed the example of Christ by converting through love and patient understanding. A gold crown of thorns, silver heart with gold rays, on a blue field.

ST. FRANCIS XAVIER, C., 16th cen. — One of the first Jesuits, known by them as ▶ "the Apostle of India," and acclaimed the founder of modern foreign missions. His emblem, a baptismal font, refers to the many conversions and baptisms he performed on his extensive travels. A silver baptismal font on a black field.

ST. GABRIEL, ARCHANGEL — This symbol refers to St. Gabriel (the word "Gabriel" means "God is Mighty"), at the time of the Annunciation, as the bearer of ◀ the message to St. Mary, (Luke 1:26-38), holding the spear of angelic power and the shield hailing the Virgin. The emblems are of gold, the monogram black, all on a blue field.

ST. GEORGE, M., 3rd cen. — The patron ▶ of England, a Christian warrior who is said to have suffered martyrdom in Palestine, during the Diocletian persecution. His shield was the badge of the English from the days of Richard Coeur-de-Lion on. It is for this reason these arms are borne by the Order of the Garter. A red cross on a silver field.

Saints

ST. GREGORY THE GREAT, P.C.D., ▶
7th cen. — The usual explanation of this
outstanding example of heraldic fancy is
that the chief bears a red roundel with gold
IHS representing the Host and red lions
guardianship, a reference to St. Gregory's
Mass. Three bends refer to his establishing:
a monastery, the primacy of his office and
reform of church music (introduction of
plainchant). All on a gold field.

ST. GREGORY NAZIANZUS, AR.C.D.,
4th cen. — The Bishop of Constantinople
and defender of the Nicene Creed. His sym- ▶
bol is an embroidered lozenge worn by
Eastern Bishops, known as the epigonation. Orthodox piety says it represents the
sword of the spirit. A gold epigonation, on
a blue field.

◀ ST. GILES, H.AB., 8th cen. — The King of
the Franks, impressed with the goodness
of St. Giles whom he found sheltering a
doe from hunters, set up a monastery for
him. The great militarist, Charles Martel
was also a patron of St. Giles. A gold doe,
pierced by a silver arrow, on a green field.

◀ ST. HELENA, EPS.W., 4th cen. — The
mother of Emperor Constantine. Her su-
pervision of the excavation work on Calvary, in search of the True Cross, is still
celebrated throughout the Church. It
should be noted that in common with all
Eastern accounts, the principal emphasis
would have been mystical. A gold cross,
on a purple field.

Saints

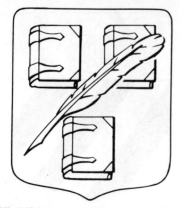

ST. HILDA, v.abs., 7th cen. — St. Hilda ▶
was baptized by St. Paulinus. At the per-
suasion of St. Aidan, she took charge of a
recluse community, was made Abbess of
Hartlepool, and later founded the monastery at Whitby. The coiled serpents refer
to the legend of her prayers changing dangerous snakes into stones. Gold serpents on
a blue field.

ST. HUBERT OF LIEGE, b.c., 8th cen. ▶
— The symbol of St. Hubert is based on a
legend similar to that of St. Eustace, which
states that, while hunting, he was confronted by a white stag bearing a cross between his antlers. A silver stag and cross,
on a blue field.

◀ ST. HILARY OF POITIERS, b.c., 4th
cen. — One of the great doctors of the
Church, the teacher of St. Martin, and a
defender of the Orthodox position against
Arian influence. A silver pen with three
gold books, on a blue field.

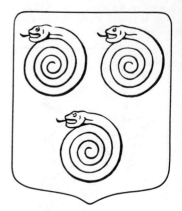

ST. HUGH OF LINCOLN, b., 13th cen.
— Saintly, statesmanlike Hugh of Avalon
was requested to become the third prior of
the Carthusian monastery at Witham, es-
◀ tablished by Henry II. He later became the
Bishop of Lincoln. A wild swan, his pet, is
said to have followed him constantly about
his house and grounds. A silver swan on a
blue field.

40

Saints

ST. IGNATIUS OF ANTIOCH, B.M., 2nd ▶
cen.—A convert of St. John, reputedly consecrated Bishop of Antioch by St. Peter, St. Ignatius was an important link between the first and second centuries of the Church. He was the writer of seven epistles as he proceeded to his martyrdom when condemned by Trajan. A gold heart with black inscription, on a red field.

◀ ST. IGNATIUS OF LOYOLA, c., 16th
cen.—The Founder of the Society of Jesus, and writer of the "Spiritual Exercises." Gold "IHS" and rays, with the letters "AMDG" of silver meaning "To the greater glory of God," all on a black field.

ST. JEROME, c.d., 5th cen.—One of the Four Western Fathers, along with SS. Augustine of Hippo, Ambrose of Milan, and Gregory the Great. He contributed ▶ courage and wisdom in his defense of the truth. His translation of the Bible into Latin, known as the Vulgate, is in general, the version authorized in the Roman Catholic Church. A red cross on a silver field.

◀ ST. JOAN OF ARC, v.m., 15th cen. (St.
Jeanne)—There is no evidence that St. Joan bore these arms assigned to her by Charles V, but they were borne by her brothers who received the surname Du Lys from the King. A descendant family displays the arms among their quarterings. A gold crown and fleur-de-lis, sword with gold hilt and silver blade, on a blue field.

Saints

ST. JOHN BAPTIST, 1st cen. — The last of the Jewish prophets, who prepared the way for the coming of Jesus Christ. He performed many baptisms for repentance. (Christian baptism is for the remission of sins.) The Maltese cross of silver, on a black field, is also the emblem of the venerable Order of the Hospital of St. John of Jerusalem.

ST. JOSEPH OF ARIMATHAEA, c., 1st cen. — The thorn cross and the Holy Grail refer to the legend that St. Joseph brought both to Glastonbury. The drops represent the sorrow of burial — indeed, anciently, the thorn itself was supposed to weep. St. Luke 23:50-56 gives an account of Joseph's service to Christ. A gold cross, silver chalice, silver drops on a blue field.

ST. JOHN OF THE CROSS, c., 16th cen. — A native of Spain, trained by the Society of Jesus, then a member of the Carmelite Order. Subject to the rules of heraldry the white top half of the cross refers to his purity of faith as reflected in his mystical theology; the red lower half of the cross refers to his witnessing under persecution. The black top half of the field refers to the color of the Jesuit cassock. The lower half of the divided field displays the colors of the Carmelite habit, white at the left and light brown at the right.

Saints

ST. JOSEPH OF NAZARETH, 1st cen. — The only record of St. Joseph is found in the Gospels where it states that he was a just man, of Davidic descent, who worked as a carpenter. A gold handled carpenter's square with silver blade, silver lily of the Madonna, on a blue field.

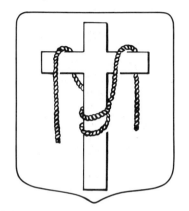

ST. JULIAN OF LE MANS, B., 3rd cen. — This saint was commemorated by the Normans; his name became popular in England after the Conquest. St. Julian's cross is an extremely ancient symbol. The reason for its choice is quite unknown. It is, technically, a cross-crosslet saltirewise, blue, on a silver shield.

◄ ST. JULIA OF CORSICA, V.M., 5th cen. — A Christian girl slave to a pagan, who refused to disembark at Corsica, while on voyage with her master. This enraged the chief of a savage tribe there, and he had her seized. She was hanged from a cross for not complying with the request that she renounce her faith. A gold cross, tan rope, on a red field.

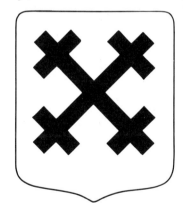

◄ ST. JUSTIN, M., 2nd cen. — The founder of the science of Christian apologetics, and referred to as the first of the Apostolic Fathers. His pagan enemies, enraged at his defense of the Faith, arranged his condemnation. A gold pen, sword with gold hilt and silver blade, on a red field.

Saints

◄ ST. KENTIGERN, B., 7th cen. — A friend of St. Columba. He was frequently called Mungo (Dearest). This emblem refers to the legend that, through the prayers of St. Kentigern, an indiscreet queen's ring was recovered from a freshly hooked salmon. A silver fish, silver ring, on a blue field.

ST. KILIAN, B.M., 7th cen. — While singing the Divine Office in the church at Franconia, St. Kilian and two companions met martyrdom at the hands of assassins. A gold cross and swords with gold hilts and silver blades, on a red field. ►

◄ ST. LAURENCE, DC.M., 3rd cen. — The archdeacon of Rome who, when ordered to deliver the treasures of the Church to pagan authorities, produced the poor and sick of the Christian community as the richest treasures of the Church. He was condemned and burned to death over a gridiron, retaining his cheerful attitude to the end. A black gridiron on a silver field.

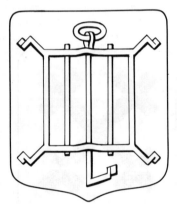

ST. LEO, P.C.D., 5th cen. — The author of ► respected theological treatises and a man of spiritual courage. Twice he advanced to meet invaders and arranged for the safety of his people. Even Attila was discouraged from entering Rome when confronted by the majestic presence and eloquence of St. Leo. A silver mitre with gold infulae, pickaxe with gold head and silver handle, on a blue field.

Saints

ST. LEONARD, H.AB.C., 6th cen. — The ▶ chains of many a sinful soul are said to have been broken through the prayers and priestly ministrations of this kindly hermit. He is known as the patron of prisoners and the sick. Gold chains on a black field.

ST. LOUIS, K.C., 13th cen. — A just king, devoted above all to serving God. St. Louis, with loyal followers, set out to crusade against the Moslems. They suffered greatly, and the king delivered himself as a prisoner to spare further harm to his men. He was set free, and later planned another cam- ▶ paign, but died before it was accomplished. A black crown of thorns, gold fleur-de-lis on a blue field.

◀ ST. LUCIEN OF ANTIOCH, B.M., 4th cen. — The dolphin refers to Christ bearing the soul of St. Lucien to Heaven. This noble servant, as he lay dying under torture, served fellow sufferers the Eucharist using his breast as an altar. A gold dolphin, on a red field.

◀ ST. LUCY, V.M., 4th cen. — This wealthy Sicilian maiden was, after torture, killed by a sword thrust through her throat. The emblem refers to her continuing devotion to Christ — an early symbol of martyrdom, deriving possibly from the Parable of the Wise and Foolish Virgins. A gold lamp, red flames tipped white, on a blue field.

Saints

ST. MARGARET, Q., 11th cen. — ►
Through her devotion to the Faith, St.
Margaret influenced Malcolm III to rule
over Scotland with mercy and justice,
while she ministered to the poor and suffering. Her feast is still celebrated by the
Scottish people. A black Greek cross and
silver saltire, on a blue field.

ST. MARTIN, B.C., c. 5th cen. — Esteemed ►
by the people of Tours, St. Martin was consecrated as Bishop of that city, despite the
objections of certain of the clergy. St.
Martin fulfilled his office most adequately.
It is believed that English armorists assigned these arms to him, having been mis-
led by a similarity of his name to that of a
well known French family. A gold escarbuncle on a blue field.

◄ ST. MARGARET OF ANTIOCH, V.M.,
4th cen. (St. Marina) — One legend understood mystically by the Medieval Church
relates that this saint, when under persecution, was confronted by a dragon (Satan)
which devoured her. The cross she wore
grew so large in his mouth that she
emerged unharmed. A gold cross and
dragon, on a blue field.

◄ ST. MARTHA, V., 1st cen. — St. Martha is
mentioned (Luke 10:38-42) as serving
Christ with refreshment. A covered table
with blue cloth and white stripe, dark
brown cups, pitcher and bowl containing
red fruit. The exposed wood of the table is
also dark brown. All on a silver field.

Saints

ST. MARY MAGDALENE, PEN., 1st cen. ▶
— As mentioned in the Gospel of St. John,
St. Mary (whom the iconographers have
always identified with Mary, the sister of
Martha and Lazarus) anointed the Lord
with precious ointment of spikenard. Hence
the white ointment pot with gold cover and
base, on a divided field of purple, for peni-
tence, and black, for mourning, bestrewn
with silver teardrops.

ST. NEOT, C., 9th cen. — St. Neot was a
scholarly monk who dwelled in a modest ▶
hermitage. Through his influence, King
Alfred the Great is said to have contributed
much to the educational development of
the nation. A tan hind on a silver field.

◀ ST. MICHAEL, ARCHANGEL — The leader
of the celestial armies and guardian of the
souls of men. This emblem (as assigned in
Harl. MS, 5852, in the British Museum) is
traditional, although the explanation is apparently lost. The cross is sometimes shown
with trefoiled ends. A red cross, as illustrated, on a silver field.

◀ ST. NICHOLAS OF MYRA, B.C., 4th cen.
— The patron of children. The Bishop of
Myra is said to have overheard a conversa-
tion which made it clear that, because of
poverty, a family was about to be forced to
sell its children as slaves. He secretly threw
three purses of gold into their house. Three
gold roundels (bezants) on a blue field.

Saints

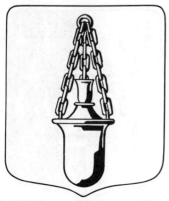

ST. NILUS, AB., 10th cen. — St. Nilus, a Greek, was the gentle, humble abbot of Grotta Ferrata, near Rome. He refused the Bishopric of Rossana, preferring his simple life of devotion and service to Christ as he willed. A sanctuary lamp of gold on a black field.

ST. NORBERT, AR., 12th cen. — A member of the court of the Emperor Henry IV, who was converted. He later founded the Order of the Praemonstratensians, a branch of the Augustinians, which spread to a considerable extent over England. He was made Archbishop of Magdeburg, Germany. A gold ciborium on a black field.

ST. OSMUND, B.C., 11th cen. — Through the efforts of this Bishop of Salisbury, many churches were erected and beautified, and a uniformity of service was brought about in his diocese. This rite, the Sarum Use, spread to other churches and was used up to the reformation. The first Prayer Book in English drew heavily on it. A black saltire on a gold field.

ST. PATRICK, B.C., 5th cen. — The Apostle of Ireland. St. Patrick spoke of himself both as a Roman and a Briton. The exact place of his birth is not known. At the age of fifteen, after a raid, he was carried off to Ireland. When released he traveled abroad, studied and received Holy Orders. He returned to Ireland as a bishop. A red saltire on a silver field.

Saints

ST. PAUL, A.M., 1st cen. — The Apostle to ▶ the Gentiles. St. Paul's symbol, as assigned by medieval heralds, is two swords crossed saltirewise. Equally suitable is the emblem shown. A white book opened to display the inscription, "The Sword of the Spirit," in black with red upper case letters, and a silver sword with gold hilt, on a red field.

ST. PETER NOLASCO, 13th cen. — The ▶ first Superior of the Confraternity of Mercy at the time Spain was in danger from the Moors. The Order was able to effect the return of thousands of captive Christians to their homes. The bell refers to the call of those in need of assistance. A gold bell, silver rays, on a black field.

◀ ST. PERPETUA, M., c. 3rd cen. — A young matron who had just given birth to her first child, St. Perpetua bravely refused to retract the Faith, when imprisoned with her loyal maid Felicitas. They were denounced for taking instruction preparatory to being baptized. A gold dragon, silver ladder on a red field.

◀ ST. PETER OF VERONA, M., 13th cen. — St. Peter, professed in the Dominican Order, eloquently upheld that portion of the Creed which states, "God made Heaven and Earth." Struck with a hatchet and stabbed by his opponents, he loyally traced on the ground, "Credo in Deus," (I believe in God). A gold sword on red section of field (line of separation shown), "Credo" in red on silver portion of field.

Saints

ST. PRISCA, V.M., 1st cen. — A Christian ▶ child of Rome, said to have been exposed to a ferocious lion in the arena, at the time of the Emperor Claudius. To the dismay of the idolators the lion crouched at her feet and refused to harm her. She was led back to prison and later beheaded. A red lion on a white field.

ST. REMIGIUS OF REIMS, B.C., 6th cen. ▶ — Through the efforts of the Bishop of Reims, the Frankish nation became a strong Orthodox nucleus in the West. The ampulla represents the vessel containing the Holy Oil used at the coronation of King Clovis. A gold ampulla on a blue field.

◀ ST. POLYCARP, B.M., 2nd cen. — The Bishop of Smyrna was condemned to death by burning. The flames refused to do their task, billowing about like sails, exposing the bishop's figure in a radiant light. A soldier used his spear to end the spectacle. Outside flame of blue, middle flame of gray tipped white, fire flame of yellow tipped red, brown logs, all on a silver field.

◀ ST. RAPHAEL, ARCHANGEL — The chief of the guardian angels who represents the High Priestly Office of Jesus Christ. The emblem shown includes two symbols of his care. A silver staff, gold wallet, on a blue field.

Saints

ST. ROMUALD, AB., 11th cen. — This ▶
good abbot, in order to change the location
of his hermitage, was forced to feign mad-
ness. He later founded the Order of Camal-
doli. The ladder refers to his spiritual
ascent. A gold ladder on a black field.

◀ ST. SABBAS, AB., 6th cen. (St. Sabas) —
The humility of St. Sabbas, the famous
Palestinian monk, proved invincible,
though he rose to great power in Church
and State. It was said that his fear of God
was so great that he could fear no man. A
silver lion on a black field.

ST. SCHOLASTICA, V.ABS., 6th cen. — ▶
The sister of St. Benedict, and founder of a
Benedictine convent not far from Monte
Cassino. It is related that St. Benedict had
a vision of a dove rising just before he received word of her death. A white dove on
a blue field.

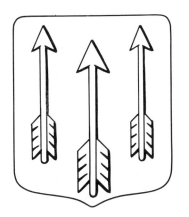

◀ ST. SEBASTIAN, M., 4th cen. — A com-
mander of the army in Milan, Sebastian ex-
erted his influence to strengthen and save
fellow Christians during the Diocletian persecution. He was denounced and ordered
shot to death with arrows, but when it was
discovered that he was still alive, he was
beaten to death. Gold arrows on a red field.

Saints

◄ ST. SIMEON STYLITES, c., 5th cen. — Desirous of becoming a true penitent, St. Simeon mounted a pillar and remained there, preaching, praying, fasting, and effecting conversions. A silver pillar, gold scourges, on a black field.

ST. STEPHEN, DC.M., 1st cen. — These ► arms, evidently of French origin, are displayed at Dijon. The stones refer to the manner of his death and the palm to his spiritual victory. A gold palm branch, silver stones, on a red field.

ST. SWITHUN, B., 9th cen. — The charges of this shield of the famous Bishop of Winchester refer to the weather legend regarding the festival of the bishop's translation. Rain is represented by silver drops on the blue chief, (top section of field). Three green apples on a silver field is an allusion to the legend that the harvest is bountiful if St. Swithun wets the orchards.

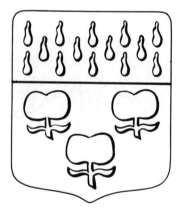

ST. SYLVESTER, B.C., 4th cen. (St. Sil- ► vester) — The Bishop of Rome, during an important period of the early Church, was known chiefly for the introduction of stable discipline. Hence the emblem which refers to his Office. A silver cross on a blue field.

Saints

ST. THAIS, PEN., 4th cen. — A beautiful ▶
Christian-bred courtesan, named Thais,
who had caused much strife among the
youth of Alexandria, expressed her shame
and was assigned the penance of repeating,
"Thou who hast made me and redeemed
me by thy Passion, have mercy on me." A
white scroll, black inscription with red upper case "Q," on a violet field.

◀ ST. THERESA, v., 16th cen. — A Carmelite nun who left her cloister at Avila and
set up a reformed Carmelite Order in Spain
and Portugal. She endured much suffering
with a joyful heart. A gold heart with red
IHS and silver rays, on a black field.

ST. THOMAS AQUINAS, C.D., 13th cen.
— This symbol, "the Sun in Splendor with ▶
the Eye," refers to God the Father. It was
through his divine inspiration that St.
Thomas accomplished his great theological
work, the *Summa Theologica,* and others.
A gold Sun in Splendor with the Eye, on a
black field.

◀ ST. THOMAS OF CANTERBURY,
AR.M., 12th cen. — St. Thomas (Thomas
Becket), the thirty-eighth Archbishop of
Canterbury, who vigorously opposed Henry
II in the struggle between Church and
State. The Cornish choughs are said to have
been known as St. Thomas' birds in medi-
eval days. Black choughs with red legs and
beaks, on a silver field.

Saints

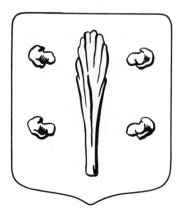

ST. URSULA, v.m., 5th cen. — St. Ursula ▶ is the patron of school girls. St. Ursula who was of royal birth is said to have traveled abroad with a company of virgins. In the Rhine vicinity they fell into the hands of Attila's Huns, and she was put to death as she tried to protect her companions. A red cross on a white banner, with gold fringe and staff, on a red field.

ST. VINCENT OF SARAGOSSA, dc.m., ▶ 4th cen. — A deacon and protomartyr of Spain, who suffered torture in the persecution of Diocletian. Top section: a black gridiron on a silver chief. Lower section: a silver dalmatic with red bands on a red field.

◀ ST. TIMOTHY, b.m., 1st cen. — The instruments of his martyrdom are well known. It was to St. Timothy that St. Paul, his teacher, wrote the two Epistles which are part of the New Testament. A gold club, silver stones, on a red field.

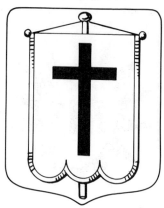

ST. VICTOR OF MARSEILLES, m., 4th cen. — This symbol, the escarbuncle, (an iron support used for ancient war shields) ◀ refers to the courage of St. Victor, a Christian soldier, who warned his fellowmen of the arrival of the Emperor Maximus, and encouraged them to meet their persecutors with a dignity befitting the followers of Christ. A gold spear, silver shield and escarbuncle, on a red field.

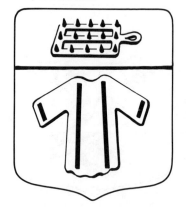

Saints

ST. WENCESLAS, K.M., 10th cen. — The Duke of Bohemia, whose designing mother overlooked him as the rightful heir of his father. He recovered his patrimony only to meet death at the hands of an unnatural brother, as he was kneeling in prayer before the Blessed Sacrament. A red banner, white eagle, gold staff, on a silver field.

ST. WILFRID, B., 8th cen. — The shield of St. Wilfrid, the Bishop of York, was assigned to him in the 16th century (c.) but cannot be definitely explained. To some, the lozenges suggest a fishing net, as he was known as a great "fisher of men." To others, the points of the lozenges refer to the See of Rome with its seven hills. Seven voided lozenges of red on a gold field.

ALL SAINTS—The explanation for this emblem is as follows: The gold crowns refer to sanctity, the gold scrolls with red inscription *Sanctus* allude to the chant of the redeemed, "Holy, Holy, Holy." The silver left half of the field indicates the brightness of the Heavenly life in contrast to the black right half and the trials of the earthly life.

NOTE: In deference to the saints and martyrs whose names do not appear in this book, the author closes this section with the all inclusive symbol of All Saints.

Crosses

ADORNED

AIGUISÉE

ALISEE PATÉE

ANCHOR

ANCHOR

ANCHOR

ANCHOR

AVELLAINE

BARBÉE

BEZANT

BOTTONY

CANTERBURY

56

Crosses

CELTIC

CERCELÉE

CHRIST THE KING
CRUCIFIX
(Christus Rex)

CRENELLÉE

CROSS CROSSLET

CROSS CROSSLET
FITCHED

CROSS AND
THORNY CROWN

CRUCIFIX

CRUX ANSATA

EASTER

ENTRAILED

FLEURÉE

Crosses

FLEURETTE

FOUR ERMINE SPOTS

FOUR PHEONS

FRETTÉE

GLORY

GRADED
(Calvary)

GREEK

IONA

JERUSALEM

LATIN

LORRAINE

MALTESE

Crosses

MILLRINE

MOLINE

PAPAL

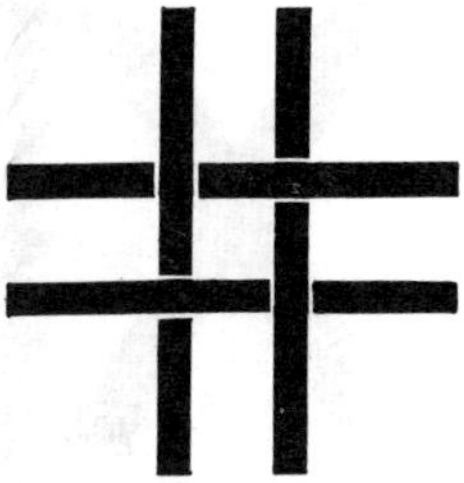

PARTED AND FRETTY

PASSION

PATÉE

PATÉE FITCHED

PATÉE FITCHED

PATÉE FITCHED
AT FOOT

PATÉE FORMÉE

PATONCE

PATRIARCHAL

59

Crosses

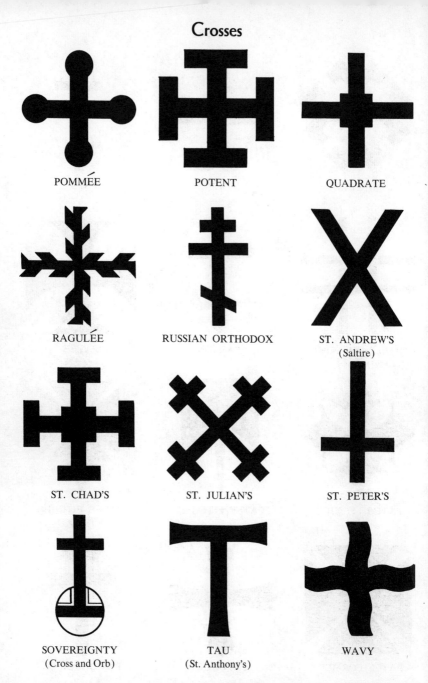

POMMÉE

POTENT

QUADRATE

RAGULÉE

RUSSIAN ORTHODOX

ST. ANDREW'S
(Saltire)

ST. CHAD'S

ST. JULIAN'S

ST. PETER'S

SOVEREIGNTY
(Cross and Orb)

TAU
(St. Anthony's)

WAVY

Stars

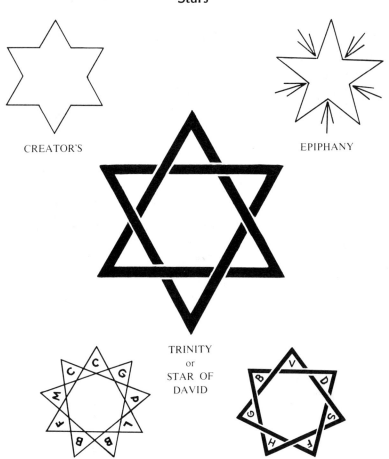

CREATOR'S

EPIPHANY

TRINITY
or
STAR OF
DAVID

NINE FRUITS OF THE SPIRIT

SEVEN GIFTS OF THE SPIRIT

REGENERATION

TWELVE TRIBES OF ISRAEL

Flowers, Fruits, Trees

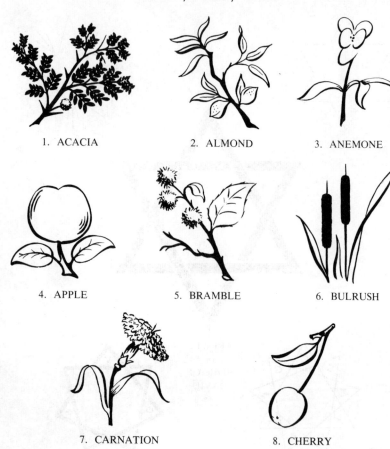

1. ACACIA   2. ALMOND   3. ANEMONE

4. APPLE   5. BRAMBLE   6. BULRUSH

7. CARNATION   8. CHERRY

1. ACACIA—Immortality of the soul. When the bush is treated with three heraldic flames, it represents the call of Moses.
2. ALMOND—Divine approval or favor. Ref.—NUM. 17:1-8 explains the use of the almond as the symbol for St. Mary the Virgin.
3. ANEMONE—A symbol of the Trinity during the days of the early Christian Church. Later, used in the scenes of the Crucifixion.
4. APPLE—Salvation, when shown in the hands of Jesus Christ or the Blessed Virgin; sin when shown in the hands of Adam. Also a symbol of St. Dorothea when three apples are shown.
5. BRAMBLE—Believed to be the burning bush that was not consumed as mentioned Exodus 3:2. (See Acacia)
6. BULRUSH—Hope of salvation to the faithful. Ref. Job 8:11.
7. CARNATION—A red carnation—pure love.
8. CHERRY—The symbol of good works.

Flowers, Fruits, Trees

9. CHRISTMAS ROSE

10. CLOVER

11. COLUMBINE

12. DAISY

13. DANDELION

14. GLASTONBURY THORN

15. GRAPES

16. HOLLY

9. CHRISTMAS ROSE—The Nativity.
10. CLOVER—The Trinity.
11. COLUMBINE—Because the flower resembles a dove, it is a symbol of the Holy Spirit. Also refer to Isaiah 11:2.
12. DAISY—Innocency as used in the early 16th century paintings of the adoration.
13. DANDELION—Appears in early paintings as a symbol of the Passion.
14. GLASTONBURY THORN—The Nativity.
15. GRAPES—With wheat, generally denotes the Eucharistic wine.
16. HOLLY—The Passion of Jesus Christ.

Flowers, Fruits, Trees

17. IRIS

18. IVY

19. LAUREL

20. LILY

21. LILY OF THE VALLEY

22. NARCISSUS

23. OAK

24. OLIVE BRANCH

17. IRIS—Also known as the "Sword Lily," which was sometimes substituted by early masters for the lily, to portray the sorrow of the Virgin for the Passion of the Lord Jesus Christ.
18. IVY—Life eternal because of its continual green color. Fidelity because of the manner in which it clings to a support.
19. LAUREL—Triumph. Ref. I Corinthians 9:24-27. Suggestive of eternity because the foliage does not wilt.
20. LILY—Purity; an attribute of the Virgin, also of St. Gabriel the Archangel.
21. LILY OF THE VALLEY—Humility.
22. NARCISSUS—The triumph of Divine Love.
23. OAK—Faith and endurance.
24. OLIVE BRANCH—Peace.

Flowers, Fruits, Trees

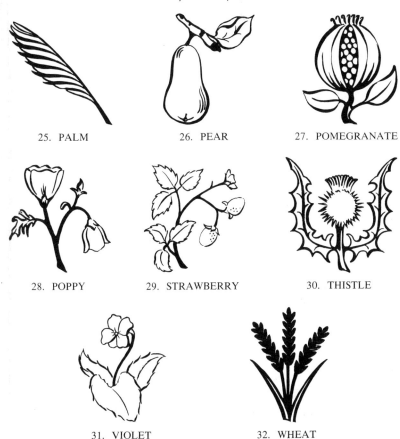

25. PALM

26. PEAR

27. POMEGRANATE

28. POPPY

29. STRAWBERRY

30. THISTLE

31. VIOLET

32. WHEAT

25. PALM—Spiritual victory. The Martyr's triumph over death. On p. 31 the symbol of St. Christopher includes the staff made of a palm tree.
26. PEAR—The Blessed Virgin. (This symbol is seldom used.)
27. POMEGRANATE—Fertility. The hope of immortality and resurrection. Because of the unity of many seeds in one fruit, it is also said to resemble the Church.
28. POPPY—Fertility. (Rare).
29. STRAWBERRY—Righteousness. The fruitfulness of the spirit.
30. THISTLE—Earthly sorrow and sin.
31. VIOLET—Humility.
32. WHEAT—Bountifulness; thanksgiving when displayed in a sheaf; the Eucharist when combined with grapes or a vine.

Old Testament

ABRAHAM

ALTAR OF SACRIFICE

AMOS

ARK
(The Deluge, Gen. 6:14)

ARK OF THE COVENANT
(God's Promise to Israel)

ATONEMENT

BURNT OFFERINGS

SEVEN BRANCH CANDLESTICK
(The Menorah—O. T. Worship)

Old Testament

THE TEN COMMANDMENTS

DANIEL

DAVID
(1 Samuel 16:1-13)

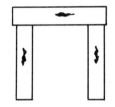

DOORPOSTS AND LINTEL
(Passover)

DOVE WITH OLIVE SPRIG
(Peace; Forgiveness; Noah)

DRAGON
(Satan)

ELIJAH
(2 Kings 2:1-12)

THE EXPULSION
(Gen. 3:24)

67

Old Testament

EZEKIEL

CLUSTER OF GRAPES
AND STAFF
(The Entry into Canaan)

HABAKKUK

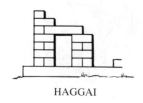

HAGGAI

HOSEA

ISAIAH

ISAAC

JACOB AND FAMILY

Old Testament

JEREMIAH

JOEL

JONAH

JOSEPH, SON OF
JACOB

LAMB
(The Pasch)

MALACHI

MICAH

THE CALL OF MOSES
(Exodus 3:2)

Old Testament

NAHUM

OBADIAH

PENTATEUCH
(The Law)

SCROLL AND WHEAT
(Pentecost)

SPREAD OF SIN

TEMPTATION AND FALL OF MAN
(Gen. 3:24)

ZECHARIAH

ZEPHANIAH

Other Emblems

ALL SOULS — From the earliest days of ▶ Christian iconography, numbers of doves have represented the souls of the Faithful. The colors are those of All Soul's Day. Four silver doves on a black field.

◀ CANTERBURY—The metropolitan See of England. All successors of Simon Islip, fifty-fourth Archbishop of Canterbury, have employed these arms which were engraved on his seal. A gold crozier, silver staff, white pall edged and fringed with gold and bearing four black crosses, all on a blue field.

CHRIST CHURCH—This shield is identi- ▶ cal to that shown at the Benedictine Priory of Christ Church at Canterbury, except for the colors. A gold cross with letters "✗" of black on a blue field.

Other Emblems

THE EMBLEM OF THE
◄ EPISCOPAL CHURCH IN THE
UNITED STATES OF AMERICA

This emblem is described in technical heraldic language as: Argent a cross gules the first quarter azure charged with nine cross-crosslets in saltire also azure.

In non-technical language it is the shield of St. George (a red cross on a silver field) with the upper left hand quarter deriving ultimately from the shield of St. Andrew (an X-shaped silver cross on a blue field, the nine cross-crosslets symbolizing the nine original dioceses are so arranged as to give the impression of the saltire, or X-shaped, cross).

THE
EPISCOPAL CHURCH ►
FLAG

This emblem was adopted at the General Convention of 1940.

The report of the Commission on the Episcopal Church Flag described the symbolism this way:

"A red cross on a white field is the cross of Saint George and indicates our descent from the Church of England.

"The Saint Andrew's cross in outline in the canton recalls our indebtedness to the Scottish Church in connection with the consecration of our first bishop. Bishop Seabury was consecrated at Aberdeen in 1784.

Other Emblems

GOOD SAMARITAN, THE — A reference to the parable told by Christ, mentioned in the Gospel of St. Luke 10:33-35. A silver oil pot, coins represented by two gold bezants, on a green field. ▶

◀ GRACE — One of the most ancient symbols of the Blessed Saviour is the anchor, which is always shown so that it forms a cross, combined with the first letter of His name in Greek (Xpictoc) to express our Faith and Hope through the Grace of Jesus Christ. Red symbols on a silver field.

HOLY CROSS, THE (The Holy Rood) — ▶ This shield or banner may be displayed by churches of this dedication. It is permissible for the arms of the cross to be extended to the edge of the shield or banner. The figure may be either that of our Crucified Lord or Christ reigning from a tree, in the ancient manner. (Illus.) A gold crucifix on a blue field.

Other Emblems

◄ HOLY INNOCENTS—The starry crown of martyrdom and the lilies of purity refer to babes slaughtered by Herod's order. Gold crowns, silver lilies, on a red field.

THE INCARNATION—The unicorn, a ► mythical creature, gracefully portrayed, is a symbol of Christ's Incarnation and his sinless life. There are many famous examples of this symbol in Christian art. A gold unicorn on a red field.

◄ THE NATIVITY—The flowering of the staff believed to have been planted by St. Joseph of Arimathaea, when he took asylum in Glastonbury, was the source of great wonderment in early days, because the blooms appeared on or near Christmas Day every year. Therefore, the flower of the Glastonbury Thorn became related to the day on which we celebrate the Nativity of Jesus Christ. (Legend has it that the original tree was destroyed by a fanatical Puritan, but that another ancient thorn, a descendant tree of the original, stands at Glastonbury today.)

Other Emblems

ST. JOHN THE DIVINE — This emblem, ▶ as used by the Cathedral Church of St. John the Divine, New York, N. Y., refers to the Book of Revelation 1:12, 1:16, and 1:20. It displays seven golden candlesticks, "The seven churches," and seven silver stars, which are their angels, on a field of blue. Together these symbols are the setting of the mystery of John's vision.

◀ ST. PETER AND ST. PAUL — The interwoven symbols of SS. Peter and Paul, illustrated here, are used at Winchester, where the cathedral church is dedicated to these saints. The gold key is always shown lying over the sword blade. Gold key and silver key, silver sword with gold hilt, on a red field.

FIVE WOUNDS — The name commonly ▶ used for this ancient emblem of Emmanuel. It sometimes bears inscriptions, under the hands, "Wel of wisdom" and "Wel of mercy"; under the heart, "Wel of everlasting life"; under the feet, "Wel of grace" and "Wel of gostly cōfort." The heart, hands, and feet in proper colors, all pierced and bleeding, on a silver field.

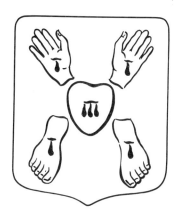

75

Other Emblems

ST. SAVIOUR — This emblem might be regarded as appropriate for churches of this dedication. It was called the shield of the Passion in England during the Middle Ages. The three nails of the Passion are black in a green crown of thorns, on a silver field.

THE WORLD COUNCIL OF CHURCHES — Shown here is one of three versions of the emblem used by the Council, which seeks to serve all men, everywhere, in the universal fellowship of the Churches of Christ. The word, "Oikoumene" is the old Greek reference to the universality of the Church. The ship with it's mast in the form of a cross, represents the Church of Christ.

Index

Index

Index

Index

3307